Emerging
from the
Heartache
of Loss

Dedication

My heartfelt thanks to all those who poured out their heart as they shared their walk through grief with me. Every experience helped shape my work.

The author wishes to gratefully acknowledge the permission granted by the following people for their contributions to this book: Beth Lawrence, Leslie Gibson, Dorothy Read, Kathy Ezaki, Lindy Kortus, K. G. Stiles of PurePlant Essentials, Rev. Maria Dancing Heart, and Sobonfu Somé for "Losing someone we love..." from *Falling Out of Grace*. Copyright © 2003 by Sobonfu E. Somé. All rights reserved.

Library of Congress Catalog Card Number: 2012046611
ISBN: 978-1-68088-280-3 (previously ISBN: 978-1-59842-707-3)

▌and Blue Mountain Press are registered in U.S. Patent and Trademark Office.
Certain trademarks are used under license.

Printed in China.
First printing of this edition: 2019

✪ This book is printed on recycled paper.

This book is printed on paper that has been specially produced to be acid free (neutral pH) and contains no groundwood or unbleached pulp. It conforms with the requirements of the American National Standards Institute, Inc., so as to ensure that this book will last and be enjoyed by future generations.

Library of Congress Cataloging-in-Publication Data

Wiseman, Carol.
 Emerging from the heartache of loss : how to survive grief and start living again / Carol Wiseman.
    pages cm
 ISBN 978-1-59842-707-3 (trade pbk. : alk. paper)
 1. Grief. 2. Loss (Psychology) I. Title.
 BF575.G7W57 2013
 155.9'37--dc23

                                                    2012046611

Blue Mountain Arts, Inc.
P.O. Box 4549, Boulder, Colorado 80306

Emerging
from the
Heartache
of Loss

How to Survive Grief
and Start Living Again

Carol Wiseman

Blue Mountain Press™
Boulder, Colorado

Table of Comforts

Introduction
An important beginning.

The most healing, reassuring words your fragile heart can hear right now are these: "It won't always be this way. You won't always feel like this." This knowledge will keep your spirit alive and help keep you plugging on to the next day. If this is your first experience with such heartache, you can cling to these words until they're true for you.

Loss is a life experience that we all have in common; there's really no way around it. And we all have to cope with it in our own way. Since we've been coping with loss all our lives—ever since we had to give up that warm, cozy place inside Mom's belly—you'd think we'd get used to it. After all, most major changes in life carry with them a loss... of the way it used to be... of the person we used to have in our lives. Eventually, we all have to adjust when loved ones die, dreams disappear, health turns sour, or relationships change. We lose moms, dads, children, husbands, wives, siblings, grandparents... our soldiers... our unborn. We lose pets, jobs, our nest eggs, and sometimes even our sanity. The volume of pain is stunning. Some have anguished for a lifetime.

Some losses are so devastating you're sure you will never be the same again... and you may not be. But the pain will lessen as you begin to adjust your life around the change.

Hundreds of experts have written volumes about the common stages of grief and our reactions to loss, but you'd probably pay just to get a good night's sleep about now. Instead of more advice, I want to offer real solutions.

During the promotion of my first book, *A Patchwork of Comforts: Small Pleasures for Peace of Mind*, I discovered how many people have been devastated by grief and loss. I was then bent on helping readers un-devastate. Through research, interviews, and my own experiences, I've discovered which strategies are most helpful to people struggling with a major loss. In *Emerging from the Heartache of Loss*, I pass on to you the solutions that have worked so well for others.

The list of ways people help themselves through the grieving process is long, but three things are clear: seek comfort, cry often, and wait. Most important of all, be kind to yourself. Running from pain makes it grow, eventually dousing creativity and sucking the joy out of life. How ironic that when we stop running, the pain softens and we can see that it will finally pass.

In an effort to help you through your grief, I have taken the liberty of reversing the alphabet in the Table of Comforts so that Acceptance, the last stage in your healing, is where you end up. You'll find crying referred to often; it's important. However, you don't have to go through this book from front to back; feel free to skip around and try out the strategies in whatever order feels right to you. Not all the solutions will apply to you, but at least one is bound to speak to your heart.

I hope you find solace in the following pages. The ideas reflect heartfelt solutions to getting you through your grief and back to living again.

—Carol Wiseman

Weep

Tears heal. Cry often, and do it well.

The word "weep" conjures up images of damsels and fainting couches and heartbroken lovers from the past. We don't hear that word much anymore, but no matter the word we use—weep, cry, sob, bawl—the result is the same: weeping releases negative feelings, recharging your enthusiasm for life… or maybe just for getting out of bed in the morning.

We all have our own style of sorrow. Some of us sob freely while others snivel quietly in a dark corner or in the bathroom with the door locked. It doesn't matter so much *how* you do it, just as long as you do it.

Stifling your tears all the time will only work against you. The very tears you may be trying to suppress are actually the healing power of your own body, so that long, loud cry might be just what you need to let this process begin. If you feel like you might not stop once you start, don't worry; tears stop on their own when they've done their job.

Talk

A built-in safety valve.

When you keep your emotions to yourself, they can build up until you're ready to explode. Converting your feelings into words, "spitting it out," opens the gate so daily life can happen again.

Finding the right words can be hard. Internal censors hold you back, making you wonder if you should say what's really on your mind. "Will I be judged?" or "Will I hurt someone's feelings?" are doubts that automatically curb your tongue. But when coping with loss, and adjusting to the changes that come with it, the only feelings that should really count are your own.

The magic of talk lets you discover that you're not the only one who feels the things you're feeling; others have felt the same way too. And by letting people into your life, you help them by letting them know *they* aren't alone either. They may not say it out loud, but they're thinking, "Whew, you too?" For some stoic souls, talking about how they feel is more painful than getting a tooth pulled. Alas, if only they knew the secret: we all feel the same inside.

Finding a willing ear and bending it will be the tow rope you need to pull yourself through your grief.

Dogs and cats have a special ear. You know that your four-legged friend will still love you when she hears the ugly stuff you have to say, even if her ears get drenched with your tears. And you can be pretty sure your deepest secrets will be safe with her.

Take It One Day at a Time

Keep life simple.

A major loss brings major change, and adding to your load by making even minor changes in routine can put you off kilter. Don't make any major decisions at a time of significant loss, as you may not be in the best state of mind. Wading through the grieving process will be simpler if you keep the routine of your everyday activities. Keeping everything else in your life as calm as possible, at least for a while, means having more emotional energy to adjust to a life that is different today than it was yesterday.

This advice is especially true for helping your children through a difficult loss. Kids need to know where they stand, and they have certain expectations every day. Keeping things normal for them keeps them in balance.

Time is a gift to us all. You can depend on it. Time guarantees change and then gives you space to settle in and adapt. Time is never finished, so you can take however long you need. Scars of your loss might remain, but the pain will wane in time.

Once you trust that time will take care of you, it's easier to wait out the grief. You might feel better next month. But then again, it might be next year... or maybe in five years. Only you know how much time is enough.

Take all the time you need to:
- *CRY*
- *Nurture yourself*
- *Connect with friends*
- *Laugh*
- *Make decisions*
- *Forgive*
- *Accept death*
- *Let go*
- *CRY*

Support Groups
Proof you're not alone.

Lots of us—of a certain age—try to deal with loss on our own because we grew up with that Old West credo of biting the bullet and toughing it out. But being too embarrassed, shy, or ashamed to ask for help just prolongs the pain. There's sure to be a better way to go through life than the hard way.

What makes support groups work so well is the mix of experiences that this small circle of strangers is going through or has been through. They understand exactly what you are going through right now, and suddenly you don't feel alone anymore. And watching the veterans who stay on for newbies like you proves that you'll eventually feel better.

A small room full of people holding tissue boxes is bound to make you feel more like letting it all hang out. In these groups, tears are common. It feels safer when everybody's crying.

Support groups are more than just chances to vent. Whining, wailing, and wallowing are essential at first, but they may keep you in self-pity mode for longer than you need to be. Learning from one another where to go from here moves your emotions along, and the shared experiences sometimes create forever friendships.

If midnight is when you're at your best, and by that I mean your worst, support groups flourish online. Shared experiences from around the world multiply the help you get: ten sets of ears become one hundred in a keystroke. The anonymity the Internet provides feels safe; your confessions have nowhere to go but into space.

Typing "grief support groups" into your search engine will bring up literally millions of results. You're bound to find one that works for you.

Soothe Your Senses
Calm the emotional overload.

You've been beaten up lately, and all your senses are in high gear. They deserve a break. If the thought of doing anything for yourself is too hard right now, consider this a homework assignment. It's important to nourish yourself a little every day because it will keep your body healthier and might even spark a new perspective.

Try soothing your senses with pleasure. Plan a whole day of sensory bliss. Bombarding all five senses guarantees that something will trickle in to help soothe your heart. Pampering the heck out of them will help you regroup.

Here are some ideas to get you started:

Taste. Potato chips could be your bag, but I highly recommend chocolate. Instead of wolfing it down, lay it on your tongue and wait: the beauty is in the lingering.

Sound. A soft tone seems logical: the trickle of a fountain, gentle curls of a calm surf, or music made for meditation. Everyone relaxes to a different sound, so find what works best for you.

Smell. Satisfy your nose with a simple selection of candles that duplicate your favorite scents. Use the healing oils of aromatherapy to enhance your mood and help you relax, or let the scent of fresh flowers soothe your sad heart.

Touch. The perfect touch would be to be in the arms of someone close. If that's not possible for you, nothing beats a bath, where hot water surrounds and soothes every cell. Better yet, get a massage. Your body will thank you for that healing touch from a pro.

Sight. Nothing is as kind to your eyes as nature. If you don't have a backyard, city parks always have a bench or a patch of grass where you can stay as long as you want. Take a moment to think about what makes your eyes smile. Is it the beauty of a garden bursting with color? An art gallery full of extraordinary images? The lapping of waves on the shore? Only you know.

For a mini-retreat that soothes all your senses at once, lock the bathroom door and start a bath. Put on your favorite music. Perch a glass of wine or cup of tea on one corner of the tub and a bud vase with a bloom in it on the other. Then... sink up to your neck in the water and stay for a while.

Sob

It helps relieve the heartache.

Holding back tears denies your humanity. Your body demands this release. I'm sure you've noticed that lump in your throat seems permanent by now and actually hurts because it's been there so long. But the lump will soften and brain function will return as soon as you let go.

Sobbing is healthy. It keeps you sane and releases pain. Sobbing out loud, alternating breaths with contorted gasps, is a natural outlet for deep emotions, so it's important to find a safe place to let them out. While you're at it, try fitting words between the sobs; talking carries your emotions, so as the words are spoken out loud, the tears will fade.

Smiles

Seek solace in a happy face.

The idea of seeking out smiles might seem silly—what could a stranger's mood possibly have to do with you? But imagine for a minute the difference in the way *you* feel facing a smile versus a face that's grim or stern or sad. One cheerfully says, "I care how you're doing," while the other grumbles, "Don't bother me!" What you need now is a soft heart in front of you.

Moods rub off. You can tell because you will automatically feel like smiling back. Is the relief you feel coming from someone smiling at you or you smiling back? Smiles beckon a better mood because they command the same from you. You might have to fake it at first. Old habits live in your subconscious, so forcing this change might feel unnatural, but practicing will help the habit stick.

Remember the times you've been around someone who scowls and grumbles most of the time and how you felt like getting away as soon as possible? Generally, people tend to avoid those who constantly show their pain to the world, so developing a smile habit will keep you better connected to the people who matter in your life.

Sleep

A restful reset button.

"I'm so tired I
can't think straight"
is something most of
us have said when we
finally hit the wall of fatigue.
Thinking might shut down at this point,
but emotions heighten, coming closer to the surface
than ever. It's why doctors often offer sleep aids
when grief is fresh and overwhelming.

A good night's sleep is not a remedy for grief,
but it's an important tool to help pull you through.
Bodies heal themselves when they're sleeping,
ironically making sleep more important at the
very time when drifting off and staying there
seem harder than ever. Even under ordinary
circumstances, you can tell the difference: worries
that weighed you down yesterday often seem less
important and more fixable after a good night's
sleep. So sleep guilt-free whenever you feel like it.
Wear pajamas all day if you want.

A good bed is not enough. You need sleeping ambiance: a bedroom that shouts "sleep" whenever you're ready to turn in for the night. Making your bedroom more sleep friendly may seem trivial and a waste of your valuable time, but it can change your life. If your bedroom doubles as an office or entertainment room, remove these distractions so your brain can focus only on rest. Get a great pillow, hide or remove clutter, and then hang something on the wall that's guaranteed, even in this tough emotional time, to make you smile.

Sing
Let "pleasure" hormones out.

Singing releases your body's precious healing endorphins, helping to reduce stress and diminish agitation. It also promotes deep breathing, boosts creativity, builds self-confidence, and feels fantastic.

If you're timid about singing because you don't think you can carry a tune, karaoke in the shower is a good start; there, you are your only critic. If that feels good, graduate to non-naked singing. When no one else is home, listen to your favorite songs and sing along. It doesn't matter if your voice is like fingernails on a blackboard, because you're alone. Don't think about how you sound—only how you feel!

What if you discover that your voice is better than you imagined? Choruses—where your voice can still be camouflaged—exist in most towns, and they usually welcome new voices. Joining a group, especially one that spreads joy to those who need a lift, can lift your own spirits as well.

"*I believe that singing can be a literal lifesaver when it comes to coping with a devastating loss, major life change, or a generally hectic lifestyle. Innately, we love to sing; as babies, it is our earliest form of communication. I've seen people's lives dramatically change when they express themselves in song. Singing can ease the crushing pain of grief, promote growth in times of transition, and reduce the effects of stress on mind and body.*"

—*Beth Lawrence, voice therapist,*
Viva La Voice in Midway, Utah

Self-Talk

*Choose someone safe
to tell secrets to... you.*

Words work wonders,
even the ones inside your
own head. The beauty of
talking to yourself is that
you are always available...
for conversations only you can hear and
comfort only you can bring.

Having so many conflicting thoughts and sorting
them out is confusing and takes time. But solutions
usually surface when the brain's debating and cajoling
is done. Admitting how you *really* feel, even if it's
just to yourself, gets it out of your system. The secret
is having the guts to admit your feelings, no matter
how irrational or indelicate they may seem. The
compulsion to censor what we say disappears when
we talk to ourselves because no one else can hear. The
trick, of course, is in the listening. Even if the answer
you're looking for doesn't emerge right away, attaching
words to feelings makes them more concrete so you
can examine them better.

Relief

You can breathe again.

Feeling relieved doesn't mean "I'm glad you died." Relief is logical to a caregiver whose life had been on edge for such a long time. Fear of how it looks to someone else might keep you from saying it out loud, but secret feelings of relief are okay too.

If you feel like you've been holding your breath underwater for longer than you ever thought possible, finally you can breathe again. It's agonizing to watch someone you love wither before your eyes. They'd been in pain for a long time, so it's hard not to feel glad for them when their suffering is done. That deep sense of loss won't hurt as much if you concentrate on the peace *they've* gained instead of the pain *you* feel.

Poetry
Words that hit home.

How do poets know us so well? The poems they write often describe our feelings perfectly. In ordinary times, when life is smooth, words oddly paired and arranged just so might not make sense. But now emotions are closer to the surface than before, so it takes fewer words to describe them.

Strong feelings drive people who have never written before to pour their hearts into their words. It's as if there are so many emotions in our guts that we can't help but spit them onto the page… whether we like it or not.

If you find a poem that speaks to you during this difficult time, make a mini-version by writing it on a quarter sheet of paper. You will end up with a tiny uplift that fits anywhere you please. You can carry this small scrap in your wallet or in your pocket to bring out whenever you want as you plod through the day. Another option is to print it on fancy paper and frame it for your wall at home; putting it in just the right place means you can draw comfort from it whenever you brush your teeth, check your e-mail, or get ready to close your eyes at night.

Do not stand at my grave and weep,
I am not there, I do not sleep.
I am a thousand winds that blow,
I am the softly falling snow.
I am the gentle showers of rain,
I am the fields of ripening grain.
I am in the morning hush,
I am in the graceful rush
Of beautiful birds in circling flight.
I am the starshine of the night.
I am in the flowers that bloom,
I am in a quiet room.
I am in the birds that sing,
I am in each lovely thing.
Do not stand at my grave and cry,
I am not there—I do not die.

—Mary Elizabeth Frye

Plant a Tree

*Nurturing it keeps
your loved one close.*

Filling a hole
in the earth with
a special tree can help
fill the hole in your heart.
As you dig, you'll not only stir
the soil, but you'll also free up whatever emotions
have taken root in your soul. Planting a tree and
taking care of this living remembrance will help keep
your loved one's spirit alive. As you watch it grow
and mature—losing and regaining its leaves and
blossoms over time—you'll be constantly reminded
that life continues no matter what.

This dedication ritual might be difficult, but
here's an idea that may help: Imagine weeping your
grief into the hole as you dig. Then fill it up with the
love of whomever you lost.

Photos

Focus on the fun you had.

Photographs (and videos) capture moments that take you back to another time. Looking at photos of family, friends, or the pet you loved so dearly helps you focus on the fun times you had instead of what you've lost. Whoever's passed from your life would love that you're remembering them fondly. Thinking only about the loss denies the time you were given together. Remembering helps you to smile again.

The candid photos we snap of each other always trigger stories of what led up to the shot: weird or wonderful vacations, tender moments together, and monumental home projects that no one would believe without proof.

Seeing the face of your mom or dad in a frame close at hand keeps them with you at times when you need them the most. When the one you lost was the love of your life, saying, "I miss you" to his likeness brings your hearts together once again. A photo is tangible. Something you can reach out and touch keeps that connection alive when you're not ready to let go yet.

As the years go by and vivid memories dim, a photo fills in the details that aren't very clear anymore. Building a memory book of your special times together means you have something handy to hold on to when you need a lift.

Permission to Talk About It

Recognize the elephant in the room.

There's an elephant in the room that people like to pretend they don't see. They work so hard to tiptoe around your loss that pretty soon even you feel like avoiding the subject completely. Maybe they think they're doing you a favor by not reminding you, but you know it's the opposite. You're dying to talk about it.

Give yourself permission to talk about the person you lost whenever you feel the need. Saying the words out loud honors your loved one and comforts you by keeping him or her closer for a little while. And remember: it's not your responsibility to make those around you feel more comfortable—that honors them instead of the one you lost. You can just be blunt and start talking, ignoring a friend's discomfort, or you can simply say, "I want to talk about it." Their reaction might surprise you.

This could be the reason young children bounce back faster than adults. They don't know there are these "rules" and usually blurt out what they need to. Take a lesson from kids, because taking care of yourself is the only way you can possibly be there when they need you.

Peek Skyward

The box office is always open.

Watching the clouds drift around, morphing from one outline to the next, lets you focus for a moment on something other than your own emotions. This sky-breather gives your brain a chance to unwind, perhaps rewinding to a better place. All you have to do is tilt your nose up from the grindstone where the drive to be busy every minute keeps it most of the time. And if you're heaven minded, sky gazing helps you remember that those you've loved who are gone are watching over you.

Once you start noticing all that goes on above your head, you won't want to miss the show: pink sunsets, silent snowfalls, dot-to-dot star stencils, rainbows, images in the clouds, and the man in the moon.

The moon itself can be amazing, with its slivers and halves and wholes, and sometimes a light so bright that you can take a walk at midnight without stumbling in the dark. Then there's that time of year, in the fall, when its size and color changes from yellow to orange, settling down on the horizon more at eye level like a pumpkin suspended in the sky.

Patience

Grief keeps its own time.

Grief keeps its own time. Wanting the pain to go away fast makes sense, but some things just can't be hurried. Instead of trying to hasten your grief along, you need to allow the healing process to take place. Waiting patiently allows the loneliness and sorrow to slowly fade away on their own.

Have patience with yourself; it will give you the time you need to feel your feelings. Have patience with others too; unfortunately, the people around you won't always know what to say or do and will sometimes hurt you with their words... or with their obvious silence. Being patient will help make sure you're still friends when all this is over.

My favorite quote hangs on my kitchen wall: "Adopt the pace of nature. Her secret is patience." Thank you, Ralph Waldo Emerson, for this reminder to stay on course. This simple phrase has been a constant reminder over the years to slow down my mind, my body, and my expectations. Developing the "patience habit" takes patience.

Own Your Feelings
Confess to yourself.

Keeping "ugly" thoughts hidden, even from yourself, seems natural at first because being mad just doesn't seem right: she couldn't help dying and, besides, you loved her. And what about the guilt? How could you possibly be angry with the very person you cared so much about?

Denial serves its purpose at first by insulating you from heartbreak, but holding on to strong emotions for a long time makes sure they fester, prolonging the agony you feel. Confusing and conflicting emotions just keep piling up, but giving them voice releases them. To move on, fess up.

Common reactions to loss are predictable, but the list of possibilities is long. There is no right or wrong way to feel, nor is there a time limit for feeling it. Be angry with yourself, with God, the doctors, the person who's gone, or just be angry in general. Be afraid or relieved or depressed. Feel numb, crazy, or confused. Remembering that we don't choose our emotions— they choose us—will make it easier to stop hiding them… from yourself and from everyone around you.

New Rituals and Traditions

Use ceremony to push forward.

The occasions you shared with someone dear are so hard to face the first time they crop up. Just when you start having fewer days when tears don't come before morning coffee, a special occasion looms large, reminding you again that your life has changed forever. Holidays, anniversaries, and birthdays hit home in a big way, but it's the smaller rituals you shared that you have to face the loss of more often: lunch dates with a friend, Mom's advice when you need it, bedtime reading with the kids, or even spaghetti dinner every Sunday. It's those everyday things you miss most.

Rituals and traditions express the values and relationships we hold dear. They keep us connected to fond memories, but there's no harm in altering them so you won't take a dive every time an occasion rolls around.

Try creating new, personal ceremonies to honor the one who is gone. This can be a more loving way to remember them, rather than remaining "loyal" by holding on to the sadness. Besides, devising something new will give you purpose at a time when you feel helpless.

Rituals to help you heal:

- *Attach personal notes to a balloon so the wind can deliver them.*
- *Create a scrapbook of memories.*
- *Cook a favorite meal and share it in your heart.*
- *Listen to your favorite song with your loved one in mind.*
- *Fill a box with painful memories and bury it.*
- *Light a special candle on special days.*
- *Donate to their favorite charity.*
- *Spend time with others who are lonely.*

Nature

*Let Mother Nature
comfort you.*

Nature works
its magic all the
time. Being away from
civilization and all that it
entails (people… buildings…
cars… obligations) is a change of
pace that calms the body and brain. It's the
reality check we all need from time to time because
life cycles are displayed everywhere in nature. Every
fallen leaf and every flower in bloom reminds us of
the way it's supposed to be. Loss is inevitable in life;
so is growth.

You may painfully feel your loved one's absence
in a home you shared, but you're never really alone in
the woods or any small wooded space. Wind rustles
through the trees, and nearby creeks provide the
sound of a happy trickle. Birds carry on with their
chirping as you pass underneath them. Squirrels jump
from branch to branch, occasionally chasing each
other around a trunk until the blur of tails resembles
a party streamer wound around just for the occasion.
You can't help but smile at that.

The ocean has its own special magic. The roar of waves can help to drown out your sorrow—the noise is so loud that no one can hear you screaming into the wind. On a fair-weather day, the perpetual white noise of mild surf can hypnotize you into relaxation.

Spending time in nature will help calm the chatter in your head, clearing the way for the thoughts that matter most to you or no thoughts at all.

Music
The power to lift a heavy heart.

Music moves you unintentionally. Without your permission, its beauty or rhythm can bring tears to your eyes or a smile to your face… even when you didn't think it possible. The sound of your favorite song engulfs your body like the deep water in a bathtub filled to the brim, calming raw emotions and aching body parts.

Dancers, of course, know this very well. Their toes have lives of their own, tapping to the beat no matter what. If you shared the love of music with the one you lost, playing something they loved might bring you together again.

The right song selection can alter the ugliest of moods and the saddest of hearts. Picking gentle music that's barely there duplicates that feeling you get on a massage table as someone gently kneads your muscles into relaxation.

Put on your favorite music. Lie down on the bed, arms and legs outstretched. Try to shut out everything else and listen for an hour. Only listen; don't think. Making room for the music to drift in gives you a break and helps a new point of view emerge.

Massage

Muscle kneading releases the pain.

Muscle kneading soothes a ravaged soul. Scented oils pave the way for seasoned fingers to glide along trouble spots. And when stress hits your life, these spots are everywhere.

Stressed muscles block the movement of oxygen and nutrients, increasing toxins and getting your body out of whack. The healing power of touch helps to balance your body's energy flow so you can better handle whatever life throws at you.

Shelling out a few bucks for that hour to let someone caress and untangle your growing heap of mixed-up emotions is money well spent. Bodywork lifts your mood so you can deal with the days.

If you're shy about baring it all in front of a stranger, you can always start with a foot massage. Reflexology tells us that toes and soles mysteriously connect with different parts of the body. Manipulation of these small and mostly forgotten parts affects the rest of your body and relaxation is guaranteed.

Knowing Someone Cares

Learn that you matter after all.

You can tell if someone really cares what you're going through. They are watchful enough to know when to leave you alone and helpful enough to assure you that you're not. Your lousy day can change with the smallest of gestures: someone asking how you're doing and sticking around long enough to hear the truth and respond, the unhurried tone of a heartfelt comment, or the comfort of an arm around you. And all of us are grateful for coworkers who pick up the slack when our focus wanders.

An acquaintance, a workmate, even the stranger standing next to you in line might recognize your pain and offer an ear or at least a smile. Best of all is the friend who shows up unexpectedly with take-out and a patient ear. And when there's no human in sight, a lick on the face from your best canine friend is love you can count on.

Simple things that show someone cares:
- *An ear or an e-mail*
- *An invitation to lunch*
- *A card that makes you laugh*
- *Showing up with a funny movie*
- *Baking your favorite cookies*
- *A shared cup of coffee*
- *Just being there*

Knowing I'm Normal

Discover you're not so weird after all.

Most of us crave to fit in somewhere, but fitting in usually depends on others not thinking we're too weird. It's why we usually keep questionable thoughts to ourselves and why you don't hear talk of UFOs or ghosts very often. But think about this vicious cycle: never divulging what's really on your mind means that nobody ever knows what anyone is going through. This silence keeps everyone in the dark, preventing us all from ever finding out what normal is. Normal is debatable.

It's easy to feel the pressure from people around you to "get over it." But they don't know what's going on in your head. Grieving is a personal journey that's as unique as each of us, so pretty much everything is normal. You do what you have to do. No rules are set in stone, just common reactions. Deviating is normal.

Some of us weep endlessly. Some of us are too angry or numb to cry at all. The list of common reactions to loss is long, but what you feel now is so personal that you're sure no one could possibly know what you're going through.

Some common reactions to grief:

anger	lack of energy
anguish	fatigue
anxiety	hollowness
apathy	chest and/or
guilt	throat tightness
helplessness	weakness
listlessness	confusion
loneliness	difficulty
numbness	concentrating
relief	disbelief
sadness	hallucinations
shock	preoccupation
yearning	trembling
absent-mindedness	headaches
changes in appetite	denial
crying	depression
difficulty making	despair
decisions	frustration
sleep problems	resentment
social withdrawal	bitterness
restlessness	hatred
breathlessness	limbo

Keep Memories Alive

Hold them in your heart.

Remembering the good times you shared keeps the ones you've lost in your heart long after they're gone. At first, reminders are salt in your wound, but the great moments you had together will start to seep back into your head after your tears slow down some.

When sadness isn't the first thing that hits you one morning, maybe then there will be room for remembering. Maybe then there will be room for a smile... and it'll feel good to smile again. Fond memories start filtering back and gradually replace the pain of loss, making sure that the one you lost isn't gone completely. What you and your loved one shared still exists in your mind, so activating those memories allows you to relive the pleasure all over again.

Maybe you have recipes from someone who has passed away. Long after the pain of loss passes, you get to remember them with a smile every time you try to decipher their food-splattered abbreviations. Or call on friends and family to compile memories of the one you've lost into a book that you can read when you need a reminder and a smile.

Journal
Funnel feelings through your fingertips.

You don't have to be good with words to write them down. Just pick the ones that apply to you and arrange them any way you please. All that counts is letting them out. Writing a letter (whether you mail it or not) diffuses anger... at insurance companies, hospitals, your sweet child, Mother Nature, God, or the one who left you when you weren't ready.

Writers already know this secret weapon of dumping words onto the page. They use it as a tool to jump-start their own wordplay. Poetry buffs already realize that stanzas are most always fed by the poet's heart... whether it's aching, jumping for joy, or pounding with rage.

You don't have to be a writer to benefit from dumping your mental junk. The idea is to hot-wire your creative mind at the start of every day.

Journaling is liberating—you don't have to explain anything to anybody. Journals don't judge or ask questions. They won't admonish you for the shameful thoughts you wrote about the day before. Putting your thoughts down on paper, no matter how out of control they seem, helps dissolve anger or sadness or fear. And writing things down that you wish to say but probably shouldn't stops you from saying something you might regret tomorrow.

Writing twice a day or twice a week, six words or six pages, will keep emotions from accumulating. If words don't come easily, drawing pictures of how you feel works just as well. The relief comes from opening the door and letting feelings out.

Journals come in hundreds of designs, so it's easy to choose one that's a good fit for you. Thinking of your journal as your buddy—with a special picture or name on the front—makes spilling your guts easier. One day you'll have a harder time thinking of something to write about. Maybe that's when your grief will start to fade.

Try a pen prayer. Write down a question for yourself in your journal. When the answer suddenly dawns on you later, write that down too. Sometimes heavenly whispers come in actual words.

Humor

Laughing lightens the load.

Little by little, the urge to smile will start to creep back. It may be hard at first because it can feel so much like betrayal: "How can I dare have fun? It must mean I don't care that you died… that I don't miss you." But sometimes you just can't help yourself. Believe it or not, laughing and crying are very closely related emotions: everyone has laughed until they cried at some point in life. If you wonder how on earth you could feel like laughing right now, remember that feelings don't have to make sense—sometimes they're just plain irrational and illogical.

Physically, laughter works the body. Blood vessels dilate, helping to reverse a temporarily elevated blood pressure and heart rate. Endorphins—your body's natural painkillers—increase. Your lungs, diaphragm, and all nearby organs get massaged. Laughing to the point of tears triggers a release valve that starts eliminating stress and toxins from your body.

Although it might seem weird to be matching up the words "hospice" and "humor," Suncoast Hospice, with locations in Southern Florida, embraces the mood-elevating effects of laughter. Volunteers from their Hospice Smile Team stuff jokes and riddles into real prescription bottles before handing them out. The labels read "Laughter is the best medicine—take as needed." This humor therapy even goes a step further, providing Comedy Carts and Clown Rounds to hospital patients.

Humor helps you to survive and get back to the land of the living. As secret internal chuckles slowly creep back into your life, little by little you'll allow these "betrayal" moments to show, and soon they won't feel like betrayal anymore. Laughing through your tears eventually cancels them out.

"One of the greatest gifts we can share with others is a smile. As families work through a loss or prepare for a celebration of one's life, it is important to share their funniest moments!"
—Leslie Gibson, RN, BS, Community Liaison,
Suncoast Hospice

Hope
Trust that sadness will pass.

Hope is something to grab on to until time has had a chance to do its work. Hope eases the present and looks to the future. Difficult circumstances are more bearable if we know that tomorrow will be better. Believing in your heart of hearts that hard times will eventually pass buoys your mood when the bottom falls out.

If this is your first time with such sorrow, it's hard to switch off those all-consuming thoughts of what you've lost—and all that it means—and start concentrating on a time when you'll feel better. Right now, that time seems very far away. This is when it helps if you're already a cockeyed optimist.

If you've been down this road before, you already know that your heavy heart will eventually lighten. You already know that you just have to wait it out and keep focused on better days ahead.

Hit Golf Balls

Channel anger through your clubs.

Why waste a good golf swing? Whacking golf balls dissipates the anger and betrayal you feel inside... maybe toward your loved one for leaving you or at friends who are avoiding you, either because they just don't know what to say or they think they have to watch their words and tiptoe around you.

Hitting golf balls around the course is cheaper than therapy. If you write a name or initials on each ball, you can send your emotions about particular people in the right direction: away. Whacking that golf ball is a safe way to hit them or even drown them in a water hazard. Some of those folks might need more than one whack, so you might want to bring a bucketful!

Maybe it's not the lush green that lures golfers to the course. Maybe it's the therapeutic release that keeps them coming back for more.

Help Others

Take a break from yourself.

Putting someone else's needs above your own serves you well in grief because it gives your own heartache a temporary rest, and helping others lets you know you're still valuable at a time when you're not sure you are.

Try volunteering for something specific that forces you to schedule appearances—a place you have to be where someone's depending on you to show up. Being around people will force you to interact when maybe all you've done lately is keep to yourself.

Causes bloom everywhere from the holes left in the hearts of grievers. Legislation reform and crusades are usually started by loved ones who feel cheated by the loss of a child or a love. You can give purpose to the death of a loved one by starting a charity or bringing attention to an important cause. Doing something positive with your grief will help you find more peace.

We all have something that someone else needs: our time, talents, advice, or a listening ear. That helping urge seems to be in our genes. We can donate ten bucks, our castoffs, and our blood. We can help tow cars out of the snow or keep tabs on elderly neighbors.

All thoughts of yourself disappear when you're there for someone else.

If you like to sew, visit your local fabric store, get ten lengths of fun flannel, put your nose to the cutting board, and make nightgowns for all the women and girls you know… and then for some you don't. The gratitude from someone who's had to sleep in her clothes will start filling your heart again. And feeling that snuggly flannel between your fingers doubles your comfort.

Have Faith in Yourself
Listen to your own advice.

It seems like everyone wants to give you advice for getting through this tough time—advice that helped them. But you're not them, so consider listening to yourself for a change. You're smarter than you think you are. The proof is in all those ideas that have popped into your head over the years or in the gut feelings that have pushed you to do, or *not* do, something. All are begging to be heard, but we keep our brains too busy to pay attention.

Most of us just go along with what's happening around us because we're all so used to conforming. Bucking the "busy" trend and following your own advice takes courage. You'll start to trust your own voice, maybe for the first time in your life, if you start noticing the good things that happen when you do.

Guidance
Imaginary crumbs to follow.

What to do... how to feel... where to go.
It's hard to make these decisions when surprising
emotions are getting in the way of logic. Decisions
are hard enough in ordinary times. Unfortunately,
the daily details of your life don't stop needing
attention because you've had to face this loss, but
asking for help isn't always easy.

Help can come in surprising ways. Maybe God
will give you a bright idea or a gut feeling. Or a walk
in the woods will give the healing effect of nature a
chance to clear your head so you can think straight
again. Mysterious forces might even come together
for you, dropping a new experience right into your
lap just in the nick of time. Positive forces like these
are harder to recognize in a busy, noisy life, so hearing
them depends on pausing once in a while to let the
chaos in your brain calm down.

God
He gets you through the ugly stuff.

Life is hard, and
we need help.
Trusting that God is
by your side through all the
tough stuff is like having a loyal
friend in your corner. It's comforting to know that
He's sitting in your heart, trying to hold things
together when everything in your life seems to be
falling apart.

When it's hard to even think straight, what a
relief it is to know someone who can. You can rely
on God to keep an eye on the ball when the big
picture of your life gets blurred. You can count on
Him to pull you through because you know He has
all the answers. It's such a relief to know someone
who doesn't judge you for the way you're feeling, no
matter how crazy your thoughts may seem.

You only need to be still long enough to hear
His whispers in your ear and feel His healing arms
around you.

"When my mom died, I had a scream in my throat that was choking me. I thought I couldn't bear it—the circumstances, the things left unsaid and undone, the image of her final helplessness. I had no choice but to go outside myself for help... I physically raised my arms, my open hands reaching upward, and begged God to just hold me up. From that moment I knew I would not drown in my sorrow."

—Dorothy Read, Whidbey Island, WA

Friends and Family
Each one is a leaning post.

A melancholy mood can turn on a dime when a lonely heart finds out that someone cares. Friends and family members can offer not only a sympathetic ear or insight but also the distraction of idle chitchat, a movie, or a last-minute lunch. Maybe… they can even make you laugh. And if your grief starts to rub off on them, shared tears will bond you even tighter together. Friends and family don't really have to "do" anything—just being there helps you to feel valued and less alone.

Don't try to be brave by biting the bullet and coping silently. The real courage is in taking the risk of letting others into your heart. Your friends and family members aren't bothered by your woes. You're probably just verbalizing *their* feelings, which may turn out to be a huge relief to them. You learn for the first time how compassionate people are when you share with them how you really feel. Maybe it's because your inner thoughts sound a lot like theirs.

Remember a time when someone confided in you. You probably felt closer, needed, and maybe a bit more important. Don't get so used to suffering in silence that you forget how honored the people in your life might feel if you asked for their help. We all need to be needed, and your friends need that just as much as you did when you listened to their problems.

Family bands together when hardship hits; it is a warm blanket we can count on. They know you best because they've seen you at your absolute worst: angry, proud, foolish, sick, sad, and sometimes with your ugly cry.

Just because your family has known you for years doesn't mean they can read your mind. Voicing your need for tears, for talk, or just to stare into space lets those who really want to help know when to step up. And if your loss is their loss, too, maybe tears shed together will magnify their worth.

Family doesn't always mean kin. If yours is close to your heart, congratulations—Mom, Dad, sisters, brothers, and aunts will be there for you. But for some of us, coworkers feel closer than sisters, best friends know us better than spouses, or an online buddy can be our best connection. Customizing the concept of family multiplies the number of shoulders available to lean on.

> *"The path to healing is like traveling a river strewn with boulders, dotted with falls, rapids, rushing currents, and the occasional calm water and still pool. Navigating this river is one of the most personal experiences of anyone's life. It is both rewarding and terrifying, and, like having an experienced river guide, the help of a friend or loved one can prevent the bereaved from foundering or sinking into despair."*
> —*Kathy Ezaki, RN, Patient Care Coordinator, Hospice Maui*

Fake It

Pretend until it sticks.

When all else fails, pretend. Moving forward, whether you feel like it or not, is what "fake it till you make it" is all about. The subconscious mind is so powerful that we have to fool it sometimes. It's where old habits hide and why making changes can be so hard.

Faking it reprograms the brain with new habits. And the only way to make them stick is by remembering what our parents used to tell us when we were young and wanted to skip a game or a piano lesson: "Practice makes perfect." Practice, practice, practice. A new way of behaving takes months to embed into the silent corners of your brain, so sometimes you have to hang in there until your fake smile becomes second nature. The feelings that come with it will eventually follow.

Believe it or not, stress doesn't come from circumstances but from all the thinking you do about them. So that makes you a victim of your own thoughts, right? But think about it: shouldn't *you* be in charge of your own brain?

Keeping your brain busy with brooding keeps painful thoughts alive, so faking for a while might help to pull you through the rough spots.

Exercise

Tend to your health for better times ahead.

Coping with grief is exhausting. Anxiety stops you from getting a good night of sleep when sleep is probably the most important healing tool you have. It may be tempting to let your own health slide when you have more important things on your mind... and when emotions start running amok.

The benefits of exercise—calorie burn, endorphin flow, flexibility, strength, a better night's sleep—apply now more than in ordinary times. Oh, how much simpler it would be just to buy chocolate or have a second or third drink. Comforting yourself with food and alcohol might seem easier, but walking, biking, and pumping a little iron all work better to ease your stress by diffusing anger and keeping your body healthy for better times ahead.

Swim to drown your sorrows. Before you jump into the pool, list all the feelings you have and make body assignments: loneliness can be stuck to your elbow, denial wedged in your knee, and anger attached to your foot. Assign shock, confusion, relief, guilt, frustration, and so on. All feelings are game. Then dive in and swim around, letting the water pull each one away until they drown. Or imagine the negative feelings jumping ship as you float in the water with your eyes closed. Either way, you'll feel freer when you get out.

Envelop Yourself in the Memory
Wear something they loved.

If letting your loved one go right away is just too hard, wearing his favorite shirt or wrapping yourself in her favorite blanket keeps you close for a little while longer. One of these days, when your heart doesn't feel so fragile, you won't feel like hugging the fabric every morning. After a while, you can fold it up neatly and tuck it away in a memory box that you can revisit whenever you feel like it. Or… if it's still thrift-shop worthy, pass the memory on.

If it's your dad you lost, putting on something he wore all the time helps you remember those warm, safe hugs you got when you were little. You always thought that shirt was the ugliest one you'd ever seen, and ooh, that stinky cigar. But now the smell of this favorite shirt and the frayed neck and holes at the elbows bring you comfort. They bring back Dad.

E-mail

An online lifeline.

E-mail makes it easy to pour out your heart when phone calls turn into crying calls. Even if you type with one finger at a time, the beauty is you can do it whenever you feel like. E-mail conversations can be deeper than in person because the time between replies gives you a chance to think about what you really want to say. You don't have to come up with answers right away about what happened or how you're feeling about it. And some things are just easier to say to a computer screen.

E-mailing means no voicemail or phone tag. You can be as brief as you have the energy for. Just a few words is all you need—only one if the word is "help."

Tears won't hurt the keyboard, so sharing your thoughts over the computer keeps the ink from smearing.

Dance

Shimmy out your sorrow.

Dance is a release, so surrender. Movement and music stimulate your body by energizing and connecting you with your spirit. Allow yourself to feel the sorrow through dance. Some tunes seem to beckon your feet into mandatory service. You simply have no choice. The guilt you feel over "having fun again" subsides as your feet start to move with the music.

Grief Dancing 101: being self-conscious defeats the purpose, so make sure no one is around. Being by yourself lets you think about how it feels instead of how you look. Listen to your body and move how it tells you. You might feel silly at first, but remember that no one's watching. Pick a large enough space, then let your body move freely across the floor. Float across the room or spin into a corner and weep. It's impossible not to feel the relief, no matter how brief.

Take advantage of a night out at a dance club. The loud music might help get emotions out of the way sooner. Anger sometimes comes with sadness, and bottling everything up just prolongs its existence. Maybe that intense kind of music is a little known secret to healing faster. After all, getting it out is what it's all about.

Dance clubs also provide a cover when you don't feel like talking. Conversations here have to be yelled over heart-pounding bass, so you can always point to your ears and shake your head when someone insists on talking. They'll get the message. Then there are all those dark corners in a club you can disappear to if emotions come too close to the surface.

Daffodils

Flowers mark the spot.

This cluster of brightness that pops up in the spring has the capacity to prompt a smile. Just when the gray of winter starts wearing thin, this small growing memorial springs up to honor who's no longer with you. Those perky yellow trumpets seems to shout, "Gooood morning!" as if little happiness soldiers are all standing at attention, demanding a howdy-do. If you plant a flower patch in memory of someone, you can imagine they're greeting you as you walk past.

The idea of planting bulbs works wonders if the loss you're adjusting to is your beloved pet. Every year, the bright yellow flowers not only announce spring, but celebrate the family cat or dog.

It's perfect really, especially if you choose your cat's favorite stalking niche or your dog's favorite digging spot.

Cry
A physical expression of your pain.

Crying often, and doing it well, is essential to healing your heart. Little bits of sadness bring on teary eyes and knitted brows, but sometimes sadness swells and settles into sobbing. That deep-down cry contracts your gut so hard that you can't utter a sound until you finally run out of breath. Then, if you're not done, you catch your breath and start contractions all over again.

In the words of a friend sharing his grief with me, "When I haven't been able to cry in a while, it seems to build up until some trigger starts me going. Then I have a great cry and feel much better afterward." If you need to jump-start your emotions toward mending, watch a heart-wrenching movie. Let the jaw quivering begin.

Consider Therapy
A safe place to unload.

Crying is common in a therapist's office. You can pretend the walls are soundproof. Even if they're not, your pitiful sounds are still anonymous to anyone on the other side of the door.

Secret feelings are safe in this little office where tissue boxes beside every chair invite you to sniffle and sob as you please. You're free to pour out your heart. You're free to confess thoughts you're afraid to admit to anyone else you know because you wouldn't want them thinking you are weird or wrong or slightly deranged.

Therapists won't judge you; it's all about the listening. Knowing for sure that someone hears how you really feel opens the door you need to move through your grief. Here you can wail to your heart's content. It's what therapists expect before you walk in the door—hence the tissue-box décor.

Connect with Others
Ward off isolation.

Most everybody's been through loss in life, so words of wisdom and comfort are floating around everywhere. Just the right word at just the right time can turn your mind to a better direction. The simplest thing spoken in the flow of a conversation can make a difference in how you see the world. An objective viewpoint from a friend or even a stranger can alert your brain to a better way or a new direction for tomorrow. But you'll never know that if you start withdrawing.

Withdrawing is easy, but in the end it leaves you more alone than you want to be. Isolation creeps up. At first, talking to anyone without breaking down is impossible. You need lots of time to cry whenever you feel like it, so being alone seems like your only choice. If your friends have never been through their own major loss, they probably think that bringing it up will only make things worse for you. Or they might not know what to say, so they start avoiding you altogether. Whatever the reason, the result is the same—feeling alone and isolated. But do your best to pursue connection.

Holding a thread to the outside world gives you an emotional breather. Lunch out, a phone call, an e-mail, or a movie all force you to stop thinking for a little while. And you could use a break from sadness.

Compensate

Replace the pain with a gain.

Making up for the change that's happened in your life gives you back some of the control you've lost. Accomplishing even the smallest of goals makes you feel stronger and more confident. Tomorrow I'll eat breakfast; Saturday I'll call so-and-so; Sunday I'll get to the market. Feeling any period of strength, no matter how brief, moves you along your healing path.

We compensate all the time without realizing it. We buy our child a puppy to help her through grieving a dog she lost, or we spend more hours at work to keep our minds off our troubles. We're constantly replacing pain with gain.

Choose to Be Alone

A chance to unscramble your brain.

Being by yourself gives you temporary respite from the demands of the day. Suddenly you have a chance to think, to ask for guidance, and to hear the inner wisdom inside yourself. It could also be your only chance to let the tears flow. Chatter is a welcome distraction when you can't stand your own thoughts anymore, but constant distraction just postpones the emotions your body needs to feel so you can move forward.

Alone time in the house is sometimes all you can get; better yet is a walk through the woods or sitting in the corner of a park. Nature has a way of consoling us... with its green, with its quiet, and with life that's mostly hidden from casual spectators. If you're lucky enough to find a pond or a creek, the calming sound of water gives you a double dose of nature's soothing touch.

Chocolate

Indulge in creamy comfort.

Chocolate: it's everywhere, it's handy, and it's divine. Sometimes only chocolate will do when the advice from all those books on grief starts jamming your brain and pain threatens to engulf you.

A friend bearing cookies on a really bad day holds magic in a bag. Not only do you have a pile of instant pick-me-ups, you have someone to lend an ear, a shoulder, and the distraction you need. Besides, now you don't have to drag yourself into the kitchen, where gathering ingredients and waiting for the timer to go off seems like more than you can handle at the moment. When you need to savor that chocolaty comfort in private, tuck a candy bar in your purse for an emergency meltdown, or stash bite-sized chocolates in the glove box or in the corner of a drawer. When only solitude will do... candy's handy.

And when you do feel like getting back into the kitchen, my friend Lindy's Comfort Brownies will be the perfect recipe to start with.

Comfort Brownies
by Lindy Kortus, Oak Harbor, WA

Ingredients
- 1 cup sugar
- 8 tablespoons butter, softened
- 4 eggs
- 1 cup flour
- 16 ounces chocolate syrup

Directions
1. Grease 9" x 13" pan and preheat oven to 325°F.
2. Combine ingredients in order listed.
3. Bake 35 minutes.

Frosting
Ingredients
- 6 tablespoons milk
- 6 tablespoons butter
- 1 cup sugar
- 1 cup chocolate chips
- 1 teaspoon vanilla

Directions
1. Combine milk, butter, and sugar in a small pot and boil for 1 minute.
2. Stir in chocolate chips and vanilla until smooth.
3. Let cool until room temperature and spread on uncut brownies.

Children

A mandatory distraction.

Extra-strong emotions temporarily overshadow all those obligations begging for attention. The numb feeling you get at first makes thinking about yourself automatic. But what about the children? Wallowing isn't an option when there are lunches to make, games to attend, and hugs to give. Even though it's hard right now, attention has to shift from you to them. The good news is this distraction helps keep you afloat until time has a chance to work its magic.

Drowning in sorrow takes your children down with you. Their needs are constant and can't be put on hold until you're feeling good again. They depend on you every day, and if it's their loss, too, they depend on you to get them through. Taking care of your kids forces you to step up to the plate.

Children also offer solace. If your own are grown and gone, just notice the children you encounter as you go about your day. Their antics and natural innocence have the ability to brighten your day. Joy rubs off.

Celebrate
A proper sendoff.

Special sendoffs in life mean final hugs at airports and fresh starts. In death, sending off loved ones in style helps you honor them in the way they deserve. A celebration in their memory is something they'd appreciate instead of the dreaded sadness a funeral home implies. Who knows what their fresh start will be, but a good party will start it right.

Planning something positive helps you remember the times you had together instead of what you've lost. Writing and then reading a little tribute for the celebration might seem impossible, but asking someone else to read what you wept through when you wrote it allows you to sit back in the audience and cry all you want. When a group of friends remembers together, the mood is contagious and the reminiscing becomes a celebration of life.

Books

Escape to the pages.

Whether you choose fiction or fact, reading is respite for your brain. It gives you a chance to enter someone else's world so you can temporarily forget about your own.

Fiction transports you to another time and place with compelling description and dialogue. Nonfiction forces your brain to focus on new information, while creative nonfiction fancies up the truth a bit. Suspense and mystery get your heart pounding, and books full of beautiful artwork bring galleries right to your lap.

Holding a book is different than looking at a computer screen; feeling the weight in your lap seems more personal and gives you more time to absorb a new way of thinking. Some books just feel good… and it feels good to feel good for a change. Those with a silky-smooth cover with great artwork are just the right size to hold when you snuggle down into your favorite chair.

Blubber

Give voice to the pain.

Crying releases emotional energy, so doesn't it make sense that the louder and wilder you wail, the faster your healing will begin?

It's "teary-eyed" run amok. It's loud and needs privacy, and it's what most grownups resist. However, if our body's natural resource is tears, why do we, as parents, tell our children to be brave and hide our own tears from them? When children can see adults cry, they learn that it's okay to express their feelings instead of struggling alone. Allowing your children to see you shedding tears once in a while makes you a good role model, especially if you're a dad. With Dad, it doesn't happen as often, so that's when kids really know it's okay.

Find a thick and cuddly pillow to absorb your blubber tears.

Baths

Surround every body part with comfort.

A bath is a warm reprieve when your life's been turned upside down. The muscle relaxing that goes on in a warm bath helps to soothe your troubled heart, and you'll not only sleep better but think more clearly the next day.

The relief of warm water engulfing my body has, on occasion, literally taken my breath away. Warm water surrounds every muscle, as if Mother Nature is cuddling them and saying, "Relax, everything's all right now."

Even if you are a shower kind of person, you can experiment. Draw a hot bath, step in, and sink into another world. You need it. You deserve it.

Making the most of your bath starts by closing your eyes and taking some deep breaths as soon as you're submerged. Remember to lock the door if you have small children who are likely to burst in. And do something about those glaring overhead lights that bathrooms always have by using candles or a small lamp on a dimmer switch. Pampering is complete when you pull closed the shower curtain to wall off the rest of the bathroom and add scented oil to the water. If this isn't enough, playing soft music may help you relax.

Art

Illustrate your emotions.

Illustrate your angst, or celebrate the beauty of
the person you've lost. Loss always means change, and
change is hard. Hard begs to be expressed... through a
pencil sketch, a polished painting, or a sculpted hunk
of clay. Plain-old pencil lead is easiest, but adding color
gives you more options for expressing true feelings.
Flinging paint across a canvas compels you to let your
emotions out, but it also allows you to keep private
feelings secret if you want—seemingly random strokes
hide true meanings from the world. Sculptors have a
special advantage: there's something about squishing
clay and the mess of sculpting that helps stir up and
spit out intense feelings faster. Those of us with two
left hands can hide our creations in the back of the
closet or save them to burn later on.

Art is a natural emotional outlet for artists or for those who aspire to be artists. Most memorable works of art have tragic stories behind them. The weirder and wilder the brush strokes, the more puzzling they are to outside eyes.

Maybe art is why children seem so free; using their fingers to move paint around the page lets feelings out naturally. And making a mess is so deliciously contrary to what Mom is always harping on.

Aroma

Your nose working for you.

Soothing your senses with aroma lightens the load of a heavy heart, even if it's just for a nanosecond. Favorite scents spur smiles: the first whiff of morning coffee, fresh-baked chocolate-chip cookies, honeysuckle.

Whether your healing path is through a rose garden or a sandy beach, your nose can guide you to a better state of mind. Visit the florist, buy a scented candle, or add lavender to your bath.

Beyond the common smells that surround us every day, serious relief comes from the inhalation of specific scents used by professional aromatherapists. Aromatherapy uses oils that are more than just good smells; these scents actually help you relax by attaching to your nerve receptors, inducing a chemical response—for example, lavender oil stimulates a calming effect.

Aromatic Recommendations for Grief and Loss

Essential oils are the soul or essence of a plant. A single drop of Bulgarian Rosa damascena has the power to heal the heart, mind, and soul and ease the pang of grief and loss.

Recommended Oils:
- *Bulgarian Rosa damascena (Queen of Emotions) has no rival for consoling the heart.*
- *Neroli*
- *Lavender*
- *Frankincense*
- *Ylang Ylang (Complete or III)*
- *Himalayan or Atlas Cedarwood (for men)*

Direct inhalation: Rub 1-3 drops in your palms; breathe in for 30-60 seconds.

Bath: Add 6-12 drops of oil to a teaspoonful of honey or unscented jojoba oil. Stir the mixture into your bath water, get in, soak, and let your heartache melt away!

—K. G. Stiles

Allow Yourself to Feel
Relinquish your brave front.

Giving yourself permission to grieve lets emotions peek through. The word "permission" may conjure up images of parents and teachers and wagging fingers, so it can feel weird to have to give it to yourself. We spend so much of our lives doing what's "right" that eventually our own feelings get lost in the shuffle. But getting through your grief in one piece depends on your knowing, for sure, that you have the right to feel any way you want. Then you can stop trying so hard to act as if everything is better or normal when it isn't.

The sooner you're convinced that crying long and hard is okay, no matter who sees you, the sooner you'll be able to get back on track. Moving past the pain is easier when you own up to feelings, no matter how off the wall they seem. There is no right or wrong way to feel, nor is there a time limit for feeling it.

"Perhaps the most important thing we can do for our emotional well-being is to grieve and 'let go' as fully as possible. We need to give each other and ourselves total permission to grieve. It's been said that if all the women of the world could cry at once, the world would be healed in an instant! How about if everyone—men, women, and children—were given the permission to cry and grieve as much as we needed, whenever we needed to? Would that be amazing? This is the kind of society and world I would like to envision. Let us be about expressing our emotions fully and courageously—happiness, sadness, joy, and grief! Let us learn to be whole and complete human beings once again."

—Rev. Maria Dancing Heart

Acceptance

Moving forward at last.

It can feel a lot like betrayal to stop feeling sad, so it's easier to hold back at first. Staying sad just seems like the right thing to do so the one you lost, and everyone around you, knows for sure that you still care. You may even feel guilty smiling for the first time since your loss. But letting go of sadness is not the same as letting go of a person, and accepting your loved one's death doesn't mean that you will ever forget about them.

Trying to focus on the happy memories keeps your loved one close to your heart better than clinging to the sadness of your loss. It also helps shore up your emotions so you can rediscover the positives in your life again. The positives are still there—they've just been temporarily misplaced.

Change is so hard, but it happens whether we like it or not. Facing change is difficult, but the sooner you can get to the point of acceptance, the less time you'll spend feeling so sad or angry or all the other feelings that have come up since your loss.

The saying "time heals all wounds" is true in a way, but the passage of time by itself isn't enough. When you can finally admit to yourself that it's just not possible for things to be as they were before, you'll free yourself from spending so much time longing for the past.

"Losing someone we love is an initiation. Our life changes. It is not going to be the same again. All our relations with other people and ourselves are forced to shift. We become a new person. Although a part of our heart breaks, the spirit of the departed remains. Through that spirit, love continues to flow, helping to show us the way, if we allow it, to the lighter states of grace and wisdom we were born to reach."

—*Sobonfu Somé*

Conclusion
Wishing you well.

Now that you have some ideas on how to help yourself through this heartbreaking time, maybe you can identify with at least a few and take the first baby steps toward healing. I know you can cry. I know you can eat chocolate! If any of these strategies work for you, the relief you feel will be, well... a relief.

When you feel stuck, you often need something to jump-start your healing process. Think of *Emerging from the Heartache of Loss* as a little traveling support group to use as a resource whenever you need a boost. The key to someone else's solace may just be the piece of the puzzle that will fit for you, helping you move forward to living again. Your life can come alive again if you give it a chance.

I know it can be hard to hear this, but hindsight tells us that every loss, disappointment, and failure brings with it the opportunity for learning and growth. However difficult it is to get over loss, you often find renewed meaning and enrichment for having known a loved one.

Grief takes its own sweet time, so patience is key— patience with yourself, with others, and with the passage of time. Every person's experience is his or her own and cannot be rushed. Be kind to yourself, and stay connected with those around you who listen with compassion. And remember: you won't always feel like this.

Blue Mountain Arts®

New and Best-Selling Titles

By Susan Polis Schutz:

*To My Daughter with Love
on the Important Things in Life*

To My Grandchild with Love

To My Son with Love

⌒

By Douglas Pagels:

*Always Remember How Special
You Are to Me*

For You, My Soul Mate

The Next Chapter of Your Life

Required Reading for All Teenagers

Simple Thoughts

You Are One Amazing Lady

⌒

By Wally Amos, with Stu Glauberman:

*The Path to Success Is Paved
with Positive Thinking*

⌒

By Minx Boren:

Friendship Is a Journey

Healing Is a Journey

By Marci:

Angels Are Everywhere!

Friends Are Forever

10 Simple Things to Remember

To My Daughter

To My Granddaughter

To My Mother

To My Sister

To My Son

You Are My "Once in a Lifetime"

⌒

By Debra DiPietro:

Short Morning Prayers

⌒

By Carol Wiseman:

Emerging from the Heartache of Loss

⌒

By Latesha Randall:

The To-Be List

⌒

By Dr. Preston C. VanLoon:

The Path to Forgiveness

Anthologies:

A Daybook of Positive Thinking

Dream Big, Stay Positive, and Believe in Yourself

God Is Always Watching Over You

Hang In There

The Love Between a Mother and Daughter Is Forever

Nothing Fills the Heart with Joy like a Grandson

A Son Is Life's Greatest Gift

There Is Nothing Sweeter in Life Than a Granddaughter

There Is So Much to Love About You… Daughter

Think Positive Thoughts Every Day

Words Every Woman Should Remember

You Are Stronger Than You Know